A TALE OF DAYS WITH MYSELF

MANALI RAJ

To the woman who used to be—
quiet, questioning, waiting.

And to the woman who are becoming—
whole, joyful, deeply rooted.

This book is our reunion.

Contents

A Tale of Days with Myself

—A Journey of Solitude, Struggle, Healing, and Self-Growth —
Written for every woman who dares to embrace her own company.

Foreword

We live in a world that praises constant motion—more doing, more achieving, more proving. Rarely are we taught to pause, to listen inward, or to trust the quiet chapters of our lives.

And yet, that is often where the most sacred transformation happens.

A Tale of Days with Myself is not just a personal story—it is a mirror, a companion, and a gentle invitation to every woman who has found herself sitting alone and wondering what comes next.

With grace, tenderness, and courage, I opened the door to a season of my life most of us fear and many of us endure in silence. A time without external validation, without certainty, without the kind of milestones we're told matter. But in that stillness, I find something far more valuable—myself.

This is not a book of answers, but a book of permission. Permission to slow down. To feel deeply. To wait with patience. To hurt and heal. To grow, not through noise, but through nourishment.

If you've ever felt lost, left behind, or longing for a deeper connection to yourself—this book is for you. It is for the quiet dreamer, the heartbroken healer, the woman who is learning that her own company is not a punishment but a powerful gift.

May these words comfort you like a warm cup of tea on a cold day.

May they remind you that solitude is not emptiness—it is the birthplace of wholeness.

And may you, too, come home to yourself, one soft step at a time.

With admiration,

Manali Raj

Preface

This book wasn't planned.

It grew quietly—like healing often does.

It started with journal entries written on sunny afternoons.

With long conversations with myself.

With questions I didn't know how to answer.

And with a longing—not to be saved, but to be understood.

A Tale of Days with Myself is the story of a phase in my life that I once tried to rush through. A phase of no job, no clarity, no companionship. Just waiting. Just silence. Just me. For the longest time, I thought I was stuck. But now I know—I was being still, and this placidity was where I began to transform.

In this journey, I did not find all the answers. Neither did I won. But I did find peace.

I did find softness.

I did find a new kind of strength—one rooted not in performance, but in presence.

This book is not a guide or a formula.

It's a remembering.

Of how healing looks in real life—messy, quiet, slow.

Of how growth doesn't always come with applause.

And of how solitude, when held gently, can become sacred.

If you are moving through a season of uncertainty, heartbreak, waiting, or simply… quietude—this book is for you. You are not lost. You are simply finding your way home, to yourself.

Thank you for holding this story in your hands.

I hope it holds you back just as gently and heartily.

Acknowledgements

This book would not exist without the pauses, the heartbreak, the healing, and the deep remembering that life gifted me.

Thank you to solitude for being both a mirror and a teacher.

To the friends and sisters who stood beside me even in my silent seasons—you know who you are. Your faith in me stitched me back together.

To the women who find their reflection in these words:

You are not alone.

You are not behind.

You are a story still unfolding—and it's a beautiful one.

Prologue

There wasn't a thunderstorm or a dramatic goodbye.
No loud moment that told me, *"This is where my journey begins."*
It was just... catatonic.

Life, as I had known it, paused.

There was no job to rush to.
No partner beside me.
No clear path forward.
Just me—in a room full of time and silence.

At first, I resisted it.
This serenity felt like a punishment.
I mistook solitude for loneliness.
And waiting—for failure.

But slowly, like a fog lifting after a long night, I began to see something else.

This was not an end.
This was an invitation.
To stop chasing, and start listening.
To stop proving, and start becoming.

I began walking through my days differently—without expectation, but with awareness.
Some mornings were heavy with grief, others lit by the smallest joys.
A cup of tea. A walk alone. A breath without anxiety.

These weren't the days I would've chosen.
But they became the days that changed me.

This book is not about reaching a destination.
It's about *what unfolds when everything else falls away*—and we are left with the one person we often forget to know: ourselves.

These are the days I thought would break me.
They became the days that made me whole.

Welcome to my tale of days with myself.
I hope, in some small way, they help you rediscover your own.

I am a public policy researcher, a listener of silences, and a storyteller of the inner world. In a season of solitude, I turned inward and found my deepest truths not in noise, but in stillness.

A *Tale of Days with Myself* is my first book—a gentle offering to women everywhere who are walking the quiet labyrinth back to themselves.

If you found comfort in these pages, I hope you'll carry that feeling with you—and share it with someone else who may need it.

Healing is rarely loud. But it is always real.

Thank you for reading.

With softness and strength,

Manali Raj

A Tale of Days with Myself

MANALI RAJ

Let's Begin to Heal Together !

1

Chapter 1: The Silence That Found Me

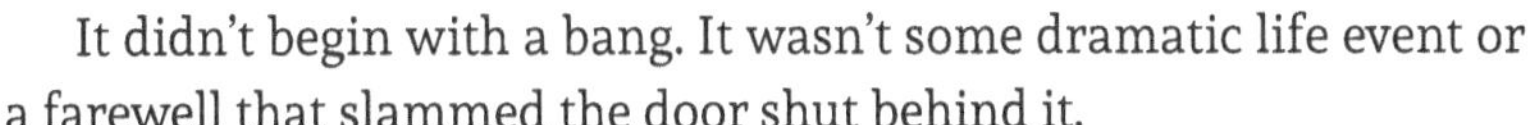

It didn't begin with a bang. It wasn't some dramatic life event or a farewell that slammed the door shut behind it.

It was quieter than that.

The silence came like fog—slow, unannounced, and all-consuming.

I didn't notice it at first. The days still passed. I still made tea in the morning, scrolled through messages, tried to smile when someone asked how I was doing. But something in the air had shifted. And then one day, I looked around and realized:

I was alone.

No job to rush to.

No meetings, no plans.

No one to text 'I'll be home late.'

No real reason to check the clock.

The silence wasn't just around me. It was inside me.

ᗡᗡᗡ

The Day It All Slowed Down

The last day at my job didn't feel like the end of anything. It was wrapped in polite goodbyes and "let's keep in touch" promises that everyone knew wouldn't last past the hallway. I walked out of that building feeling like I was forgetting something—but it wasn't a file or a farewell card.

It was my rhythm.

That invisible thread that tied my worth to my work had snapped. I didn't know it yet, but I was about to meet the person I had been ignoring for years: myself.

And she was quiet. Very, very quiet.

ᐅᐅᐅ

The Noise I Created

The first few days, I fought the quietude.

I turned the TV on just to hear voices. I called old friends under the pretence of "checking in." I scrolled through reels until my eyes ached. I cleaned every surface in my apartment twice.

Anything to avoid sitting in that silence.

Because silence, I thought, meant failure. Loneliness. Rejection. I associated quiet with being left behind. And worst of all, I was afraid of what I might hear if I listened too closely.

You know that feeling? When the world slows down and suddenly, all the thoughts you'd buried start tapping at your door?

Mine weren't knocking. They were banging.

ᐅᐅᐅ

The Night I Broke Down

It was a Tuesday night. I hadn't done anything special that day—just another loop of nothing. But that night, I lay on my bed staring at the ceiling fan, and the tears came without warning.

It wasn't a sob. It was a quiet weeping—the kind that trickles from the corner of your eye without you even realizing.

I didn't cry because something had happened. I cried because nothing had.

And in that emptiness, I felt everything. Every little piece of me that I had ignored for the sake of being "productive" or "strong" or "in control" suddenly showed up like uninvited guests. Memories I hadn't replayed in years. Doubts I had buried. Dreams I had postponed.

I whispered to myself, "What is happening to me?"

But deep down, I knew.

This was the beginning of something. Something tender. Something terrifying.

⊳⊳⊳

Meeting Myself

The next morning, I stood in front of the mirror and truly looked.

Not to fix my hair. Not to check for any pimples. But to really *look*.

And I didn't recognize her.

Who was this girl with the tired eyes and the tight jaw? Who had she been pleasing for so long? Why did she carry so much weight on her shoulders?

I looked closer. And for the first time, I didn't judge her. I didn't scold her for not "having it all together." I just stood there with her.

I said, softly, "I see you."

It felt like a promise.

⊳⊳⊳

Learning the Language of Stillness

Something shifted after that.

I stopped trying to "fill the day." Instead, I began listening.

To my body—when it was tired, when it craved a walk, when it wanted to dance.

To my thoughts—without rushing to fix or silence them.

To the breeze outside my window.

To my heartbeat.

There's a beautiful thing that happens when you stop running from yourself. At first, you hear only the noise: insecurities, fears, regrets. But if you sit long enough, if you're gentle enough, the deeper voice begins to rise.

The one that says: *"You're not broken. You're just beginning again."*

ᚦᚦᚦ

Small Joys, Slow Days

The pace of my days became slower. Softer.

I started making morning chai not just for caffeine, but as a ritual. I noticed how the steam curled like poetry. How the first sip warmed more than just my hands.

I walked barefoot on the balcony. I read pages without checking my phone. I made playlists that made me feel alive, even if I danced alone.

And I began writing again.

Not for an audience. Not for validation. Just for me.

One day, I wrote in my journal: *"Maybe this silence isn't a punishment. Maybe it's an invitation."*

And I cried when I wrote it. Because I believed it.

ᚦᚦᚦ

The Lies We Believe

Here's what society tells us, especially as women:

- "You must always be achieving something."
- "You must always have a plan."
- "You must always look like you're fine."
- "Being alone is a sign of failure."

But in those quiet weeks, I started to unlearn all of that.
Being still wasn't lazy.
Being alone wasn't failure.
Being unsure wasn't weakness.
It was healing.
It was remembering.
It was becoming.

ᐅᐅᐅ

A Letter to the Girl Who Feels Alone

If you're reading this chapter and you're in a season of silence—this is for you.
To the girl who just lost her job, or her relationship, or her direction...
To the girl whose phone has been too quiet...
To the girl who's scared of her own thoughts...
I want you to know:
Silence is not the end of your story.
It's the beginning of a softer chapter. A deeper one. The one where you stop chasing and start becoming.
Give yourself permission to do nothing.
To rest.
To cry.
To be.
You don't have to prove your worth in productivity.
You don't have to earn your healing.
You just have to stay.

Stay with yourself.
Hold your own hand.
Breathe.
There is wisdom in the stillness.
And you are allowed to take your time.

ᐅᐅᐅ

Closing Reflection

I once feared silence like it was a storm.
But I've learned: storms cleanse.
Silence doesn't just take. It gives.
It gave me back my breath.
My rhythm.
My self.
And it can give you that too.
So tonight, if the silence feels heavy, just remember—
you're not empty.
You're sacred space.
A garden before the bloom.

ᐅᐅᐅ

What is the silence in your life trying to tell you right now?
Sit with it. Listen. Write without editing.

2

Chapter 2: Waiting with an Open Heart

I've always believed in love.

Not the movie version with perfect lighting and background music, but the soul kind. The kind that sees you in your worst days and stays. The kind that feels like home and yet still sets you free.

And so, when life went quiet—when I found myself alone, jobless, directionless—the one thing that kept flickering in the corners of my heart was the hope that maybe, just maybe, love would come.

Someone would find me.

Hold me.

Save me from this ache of waiting.

ᗪᗪᗪ

The Ache Beneath the Quiet

Waiting is a strange kind of pain. It doesn't stab like heartbreak or burn like anger. It lingers, soft and quiet, like a song playing in the background that you can't turn off.

I remember evenings when I'd sit with my tea, staring at my phone.

No new messages.

I remember seeing couples walking hand in hand and feeling a mix of warmth and sorrow. Not jealousy—just a deep, slow yearning. A whisper: *"When is it my turn?"*

I wasn't desperate. I wasn't begging. I just... ached.

There's a softness to waiting that no one talks about. It's not always dramatic. Sometimes it just looks like hoping in silence. Like setting an extra plate in your heart, even when you dine alone.

ᗒᗒᗒ

The Fantasies We Hold

Some nights, I would close my eyes and imagine them.

What they'd look like. How they'd speak. How they'd understand the parts of me I struggled to explain.

In those private daydreams, I was seen. Chosen. Held.

But if I'm being honest—those fantasies were also hiding places.

They gave me an escape from my loneliness, yes. But they also gave me an excuse to not fully live. To not risk. To not open my heart in the now. I told myself I was "waiting for love," but really, I was scared.

Scared of rejection. Scared of being vulnerable again. Scared of not being enough.

So I hid behind hope. Dressed it up in poetry and prayer. And told myself the waiting was holy.

But deep inside, I was starting to feel stuck.

ᗒᗒᗒ

Love, as a Mirror

One morning, I wrote in my journal:

"Am I waiting for love, or am I afraid to live without it?"

The question sat with me all day. It followed me to the kitchen, the balcony, the shower. I didn't know the answer. All I knew was—I had paused my life, expecting someone else to press play.

And that realization hit harder than any heartbreak ever had.

I wasn't broken. I was just paused. Holding my breath. Believing that my story hadn't *really* started until someone entered it.

But what if I was wrong?

ᗺᗺᗺ

The Moment It Shifted

It wasn't a grand revelation. No spiritual awakening. No motivational quote on Instagram.

It was an afternoon. Quiet and ordinary.

I was watering my plants. The sun was soft, the breeze gentle. And suddenly, I felt... okay.

Not amazing. Not "healed."

Just okay.

Like maybe, I didn't need to be rescued. Like maybe, this waiting could be something more than longing.

Maybe, it could be preparation.

Maybe, I could stop waiting *for* someone—and start growing *into* someone.

Someone who didn't need love to feel full. Someone who *was* love, even in her aloneness.

ᗺᗺᗺ

Becoming the Love, I Waited For

That shift didn't mean I gave up on romance. I still dream of partnership, of building something tender and true with someone one day.

But I stopped starving for it.

Instead, I began nourishing myself. Slowly. Deliberately.

I took myself on quiet walks and noticed the way trees swayed when no one was looking.

I started cooking meals just for me—and lighting candles like I had company.

I wore my favorite clothes even when I had nowhere to go.

I stopped dressing for the idea of "someone" and started adorning myself because I deserved beauty.

I read books that fed my mind.

I journaled like I was writing letters to my future self.

And most importantly, I forgave myself for all the times I thought I was unlovable just because I was alone.

ᕈᕈᕈ

Redefining the Wait

There's something freeing about turning your waiting into *welcoming.*

Instead of pacing the floor, you begin to prepare the space within you.

You clean up the resentment.
You sweep away the doubts.
You open the windows of your heart.
And you light a lamp—not to attract someone, but to honor yourself.

You say to life: *"I am ready. Not needy. Just ready."*

And when you're ready in that way, everything shifts. Love stops being a rescue mission. It becomes a celebration.

You're no longer hoping someone will fill your cracks.

You're holding yourself so fully that when love does come, it overflows.

ᕈᕈᕈ

Finding Love in New Places

I used to think love was a person.

Now I know—love is an energy.

It's the way I talk to myself when I'm hurting.

It's the way I sit with a friend and hold space for him.

It's the way I listen to music and feel every lyric.

It's the way I wake up and thank my body for carrying me.

It's the way I don't abandon myself anymore.

And when I realized that—truly realized that—I stopped feeling alone.

Because love wasn't missing. It was already here. In me. Around me.

Everywhere.

ᙏᙏᙏ

A Letter to the Girl Still Waiting

Sweet one,

If you're still waiting, I see you.

If you wake up hoping today is the day someone will see your heart and stay—I see you.

If you're tired of pretending you're fine, of being "strong," of holding space for everyone else while silently hoping someone will finally hold space for you—I see you.

And I want you to know:

You are not forgotten.

You are not unlovable.

You are not behind.

You are becoming.

And while you wait, you are allowed to live. To laugh. To create. To rest. To grow. To shine.

Don't press pause on your joy just because someone hasn't arrived yet.

Build your life so beautifully that love will feel lucky to join it.
Because it will.
Love will come.
But more importantly—you're already here.
And that's enough.

ᗯᗯᗯ

? Closing Reflection

I used to think waiting meant standing still.
Now I know—it means *becoming*.
    And with each passing day, I am becoming softer.
Wiser.
More whole.
    The kind of woman who no longer waits with a heavy heart.
    But with an open one.

ᗯᗯᗯ

? Journaling Prompt

What are you waiting for in your life right now?
And how can you start *preparing* for it instead of *aching* for it?
    Write it down. No judgment. Just honesty.

3

Chapter 3: The Mirror and the Mind

There was a time I couldn't look in the mirror for more than a few seconds.

Not because I hated the way I looked, but because I was afraid of what I'd find staring back.

The reflection didn't just show my face—it held the weight of my doubts, the stories I told myself, the echoes of every unkind word I'd ever believed.

When I stood there—alone, jobless, healing, raw—I didn't just see a woman.

I saw *everything I thought I wasn't.*

Not successful enough.

Not beautiful enough.

Not strong enough.

Not "together" enough.

And that voice in my mind? It whispered every fear I never dared to say out loud.

But this chapter isn't about staying in that darkness.

It's about turning on the light.

♭♭♭

The Quiet Cruelty of Self-Talk

It's strange how easily we believe the worst things about ourselves.

The world doesn't always have to break us—sometimes, we do that job ourselves. With our own thoughts. With our own judgment.

I remember waking up some mornings and the first thought that came to me wasn't gentle or loving. It was, "You're wasting your life."
Not "Good morning."
Not "You're trying."
Just criticism, sharp and cold, like glass on bare feet.

I would scroll through social media and see others thriving—traveling, getting promotions, falling in love—and my mind would spiral.

What's wrong with me?
Why can't I figure it out?
Maybe I'm just not enough for this world.

That voice—the inner critic—isn't just mean. It's *convincing*.

It uses your own insecurities as weapons. And worst of all, it sounds like *you*.

ᚦᚦᚦ

Meeting Myself for the First Time

The mirror became my battleground. But also, strangely, my place of awakening.

One night, during one of my loneliest phases, I did something different.

I stood in front of the mirror.

No makeup. No filters. No distractions.

Just me.

I stared for a long time—until the self-criticism started to get loud, and then... something shifted.

I said out loud, *"I don't know why I'm being so harsh. I wouldn't speak to a friend like this."*

And that one sentence broke something open.

It made me realize: I had spent years becoming a friend to others... while being a bully to myself.

So I started talking to my reflection differently.

Awkwardly at first. Then with more care.

I told her:

"You are trying."

"You are growing."

"You are not a failure."

"You are enough, even now."

It didn't fix everything. But it softened something.

And in that softness, healing began.

ppp

Rewriting the Stories in My Mind

Our thoughts are like seeds. What we plant, we grow.

And I had been planting doubts, shame, fear.

So I started choosing new thoughts.

Not fake affirmations.

But *truthful* ones.

Like:

"I may not have all the answers, but I'm allowed to figure them out slowly."

"My value is not measured by how productive I am today."

"Even in my mess, I am worthy of kindness."

I didn't just think these things once and become healed. I had to *train* my mind—like a muscle that had forgotten how to lift itself up.

And each time I caught a negative thought, I gently questioned it.

Is this true?

Would I say this to someone I love?

What would a loving voice say instead?

It felt awkward. Like learning to walk again.

But with time, my mind became quieter. Kinder.

More like a friend. Less like a judge.

ᐅᐅᐅ

The Power of Stillness

One of the most powerful things I did during this phase was create silence.
Not scrolling. Not numbing. Not distracting.
Just… stillness.
I would sit by the window, close my eyes, and breathe.
No goals. No expectations.
And in that stillness, I began to notice something:
The voice in my mind wasn't always mine.
Some of it was inherited—from society, from old wounds, from other people's opinions.
And once I could see that clearly, I started letting those voices go.
I stopped carrying words that were never mine to hold.
And in that empty space, I began to hear my *real* voice.
Soft. Steady. Loving.
It said, *"You're doing okay."*
And sometimes, that was enough to carry me through the day.

ᐅᐅᐅ

Reclaiming the Mirror

It took time, but one day I looked in the mirror and smiled.
Not because I looked "better." But because I finally saw *me*.
The girl who had stayed.
The woman who had kept walking.
The soul who had fallen, cried, grown, and stood back up.
The mirror no longer felt like a place of shame.
It became a place of presence.
Of truth.

Of grace.

I had reclaimed it—not as a measure of beauty or success—but as a meeting point between who I was and who I was becoming.

ϼϼϼ

A Note on Comparison

There's something else I learned along the way:

Comparison is a thief with soft hands.

It sneaks in while you're vulnerable, and suddenly you're measuring your messy beginning against someone's polished middle.

When I compared, I shrank.

When I honored my own path, I grew.

So I started replacing comparison with compassion.

Instead of, *"Why am I not there yet?"* I said, *"Look how far I've come."*

Instead of, *"They're ahead of me,"* I said, *"We're on different journeys, and both are valid."*

Because healing is not a race. And growth isn't a competition.

It's a coming home.

To yourself.

At your own pace.

ϼϼϼ

The Mind as a Garden

If there's one metaphor that helped me most, it was this:

My mind is a garden.

Whatever I water—grows.

So I began watering kindness.

Watering hope.

Watering joy in small things.

Watering forgiveness—for my past, for my pace, for my process.

And slowly, the weeds of doubt began to thin out.

New thoughts bloomed. New beliefs rooted.

And my inner world—once so harsh—became a place I no longer feared being alone in.

ᚦᚦᚦ

Final Thoughts: Learning to Like Myself

Falling in love with yourself is a popular idea. But sometimes, *liking* yourself is a bigger win.

I didn't wake up one day and say, "I love myself."

But I did start saying:

"I'm proud of how I handled that."

"I like how I care for people."

"I admire how I keep showing up."

And from liking... came loving.

So if you're reading this and struggling with the voice in your mind—start small.

Don't force love.

Begin with respect.

Begin with understanding.

Begin with saying, "I may not feel okay today. But I still choose to be kind to myself."

That's the beginning of everything.

ᚦᚦᚦ

? Closing Reflection

The mirror is no longer my enemy.

It is my witness.

And the mind? It is no longer my cage.

It is my companion.

Together, we are learning.
And becoming.

ᐅᐅᐅ

? Journaling Prompt

   What is one thought you often repeat to yourself that holds you back?
What would a gentler version of that thought sound like?
Write it down. Then say it to yourself—like you mean it.

4

Chapter 4: Small Joys, Quiet Victories

---❦---

Healing is not a grand event.

It is not always a bold decision or a sweeping change.

Sometimes, healing tiptoes into your life in the form of the *mundane.* In moments so quiet, you almost miss them. In joys so small, they go unnoticed—unless you're paying close attention.

This chapter is a love letter to those gentle moments. The ones that held me together when everything else was falling apart. The ones that taught me: joy doesn't have to be loud to be real. And progress doesn't have to be public to be powerful.

❧❧❧

A Cup of Tea and the Beginning of Change

There was one morning I remember vividly—not because something huge happened, but because *nothing* did.

I was jobless. Alone. Stuck in a loop of uncertainty.

But I made myself a cup of tea.

It sounds so simple, almost laughable. But for the first time in days, I didn't rush it. I waited for the water to boil. I noticed the steam. I held the cup in both hands and just *sat* with it.

And in that stillness, something shifted.

The tea didn't solve my problems. But it anchored me. It reminded me I was still here. That I could still show up for myself in small ways. That maybe... that was enough for now.

The Invisible Work of Healing

Nobody claps for you when you eat a full meal after days of no appetite.

No one gives you an award for taking a shower when your heart feels heavy.

There's no medal for saying "no" to a toxic thought and "yes" to rest.

But *you know*. Deep down, you know those moments matter.

So many of my quiet victories happened behind closed doors:

- Waking up without dread.
- Cleaning my room after weeks of disarray.
- Writing in my journal even when I had no words.
- Smiling at myself in the mirror without flinching.

These are not social media updates. They are soul wins. And they count more than we give them credit for.

Tiny Rituals, Big Shifts

I started creating tiny rituals—not out of obligation, but out of self-kindness.

I lit a candle every night before sleep.

I played soft music while folding clothes.

I opened my window first thing every morning, no matter how I felt inside.

These rituals became sacred. They gave my days a shape. They whispered: *You're allowed to find peace in small places.*

They weren't productivity hacks. They were healing habits.

And they taught me: taking care of myself wasn't about being perfect. It was about being present.

ᗅᗅᗅ

Joy Without Performance

For so long, I had connected joy with accomplishment.

A good grade. A new job. A compliment. A result.

But in my quiet season, those things were missing. And joy, I thought, had left too.

Until I began to notice joy wasn't gone—it was just *different.*

It was in the way the sunlight hit my floor.

In the smell of clean bedsheets.

In the way my body felt after a long stretch.

These joys didn't demand anything from me. They simply arrived—and all I had to do was notice.

That changed everything.

ᗅᗅᗅ

Letting Go of "Big Moment" Pressure

I had grown up on a steady diet of dramatic transformation stories.

The "rock bottom to success" tales. The "aha" moments that changed everything overnight.

So I kept waiting for my *big moment.*

But healing, for me, wasn't an explosion. It was a slow, quiet unfolding.

I didn't wake up one day and feel "healed."

I woke up many days still aching—but a little less than the day before.

And in time, I learned this: small steps taken in love lead to big shifts rooted in grace.

ᐧᐧᐧ

Reclaiming My Relationship With Time

Time used to feel like a threat.

Each day I didn't "figure out my life" felt wasted.

But through small joys, I found a new rhythm.

I stopped asking, *What did I achieve today?*

I started asking, *What did I notice today?*

What did I enjoy? What felt soft? What made me smile, even for a second?

Time became a friend again. A gentle container for growth, not a countdown clock for pressure.

ᐧᐧᐧ

When the Hard Days Return

Of course, not every day was joyful.

There were relapses—into sadness, loneliness, restlessness.

But on those days, I had my toolkit.

I knew I could go back to my tea. My candle. My music. My breath.

These small joys became emotional anchors. They didn't erase the pain, but they gave me something to hold on to. Something real.

And that's what made them victorious.

ᐧᐧᐧ

The Strength of Still Being Here

If you're reading this and you've made your bed, cooked yourself a meal, or simply *chosen* to keep going—you've already won something.

You've chosen life.

You've chosen to stay.

And that quiet decision, repeated over and over, is the most powerful kind of resilience.

We don't need to prove our strength through noise.

Sometimes, the strongest ones are the ones still showing up—tender, tired, but present.

ᔕᔕᔕ

Closing Thoughts: Gentle Is Strong Too

We live in a world that celebrates the loudest, fastest, and biggest.

But this chapter is for the gentle ones.

The slow healers. The quiet rebuilders. The people who find beauty in candlelight and morning walks and folding laundry.

You are not behind.

You are not small.

You are not invisible.

Your small joys are sacred.

Your quiet victories are real.

Keep collecting them. They're proof that something within you is still choosing love.

ᔕᔕᔕ

? Journaling Prompt

Think back on this week. What are three small joys or quiet victories you experienced?

· Maybe it was drinking water mindfully.

- Maybe it was saying no when you wanted to people-please.
- Maybe it was simply getting out of bed.

Now write about them as if they were big, beautiful achievements—because they are.

5

Chapter 5: Learning to Be My Own Safe Place

There was a time I searched for safety in the eyes of other people.

In their promises.

In relationships.

In career titles and busy schedules.

In conversations and text messages that temporarily dulled my fear.

But one by one, those things would slip away.

The job ended. The conversation went silent. The support I depended on became unavailable.

And suddenly, I was left with *me*.

Just me. In a room, in a city, in a life that felt unfamiliar and uncertain.

I cried the kind of cry that feels too big for your chest.

And then I asked a question I never thought to ask before:

"What if the safety I'm looking for isn't out there... but in here?"

ﬔﬔﬔ

When Nothing Outside Feels Steady

There's a kind of ache that doesn't always come from loss. Sometimes, it comes from the *absence of certainty*.

I remember waking up in the quiet of my apartment one day, with no job to go to, no messages on my phone, and no idea what came next.

For a moment, I panicked.

Where do I go? Who do I turn to? What do I *do*?

And then I just... breathed.

I placed a hand on my chest and said out loud, "You're okay. You're safe with me."

It felt awkward at first. Silly, even.

But I kept doing it—again and again.

And eventually, that voice inside me grew stronger. Softer. Kinder.

It started to sound like *home*.

ᐅᐅᐅ

What Does Emotional Safety Actually Feel Like?

We often think safety means "nothing bad ever happens." But I've learned that real emotional safety isn't about control—it's about *presence*.

Safety is...

- Knowing that your feelings are allowed to exist.
- Trusting that you will be gentle with yourself when you're hurting.
- Letting yourself be messy, uncertain, scared—and still worthy of love.

I used to silence my emotions because I thought they made me weak.

Now, I see them as signals that I need care. And *I* can give that care.

That shift changed everything.

ᐅᐅᐅ

Listening Without Fixing

One of the hardest lessons I had to learn was how to sit with my pain without rushing to fix it.

We're so used to patching things up.
We say, *"It's not that bad,"* or *"Others have it worse,"* or *"Just be positive."*

But I began practicing something new: just *listening* to myself. Without judgement. Without shame. Without trying to be "better."

When I felt anxious, I'd sit down, close my eyes, and simply ask,
"What's hurting, love?"
And then I'd let the answers come.

Sometimes it was loneliness.
Sometimes it was fear.
Sometimes it was exhaustion.

And every time, I responded with the kind of warmth I used to wait for from others.

"You're allowed to feel this."
"I'm here with you."
"We'll get through it together."

Over time, my inner world became a gentler place to live.

Boundaries: The Architecture of Safety

Becoming your own safe place also means protecting your peace.

I used to let people's opinions, moods, and expectations crash through me like waves.
If someone was upset, I blamed myself. If someone withdrew, I panicked.

But emotional safety requires boundaries—kind ones.
I had to learn:

- It's okay to say no.

- It's okay to pause a conversation that's draining you.
- It's okay to protect your time, your energy, and your heart.

Every time I chose a boundary, I reminded myself:
"I am allowed to protect what I'm healing."
And every time, I felt just a little more rooted inside myself.

ᛈᛈᛈ

Safety in the Body

Our minds carry pain, but so do our bodies.

I used to live mostly in my head—analyzing, worrying, overthinking.

But when I started listening to my body, I realized it was always speaking to me.

Tight chest? I need comfort.
Heavy shoulders? I need rest.
Tense jaw? I need softness.

So I started tending to my body like I would a beloved friend.

- Stretching slowly in the mornings.
- Taking long walks.
- Placing one hand on my belly and the other on my heart, just to say: "I'm here. I've got you."

This physical presence brought a new kind of safety. Not just emotional, but embodied.

ᛈᛈᛈ

Little Rituals of Safety

I began to shape my environment to mirror what I was building inside.

I made my bed in the morning, not out of discipline, but to tell myself: *You deserve order.*

I lit candles at night, not for the aesthetic, but to remind myself: *You deserve warmth.*

I drank my tea slowly, wrote down my dreams, played music that made my heart feel soft.

These were not luxuries. They were love letters to myself.

Each one saying, *"You are worth being cared for, right here, right now."*

ᐅᐅᐅ

Reparenting Myself

There were things I needed to hear as a child that I never did.

Things like:

- "You're not too much."
- "You don't have to earn love."
- "You're safe now."

So I began saying them to myself.

I'd imagine little-me sitting beside grown-up-me. And I'd say everything I wish someone had said to her.

At first it felt silly. Then it felt powerful.

Then it felt necessary.

That's how I began *reparenting* myself.

And in doing so, I became my own protector, nurturer, and guide.

ᐅᐅᐅ

The Day I Realized I Had Changed

I remember one particularly hard day.

Something I'd hoped for didn't work out. The old version of me would have spiraled—questioned everything, blamed herself, shut down emotionally.

But this time, I sat quietly. I let the tears come. And then I made dinner. Watched a movie. Lit my candle.

I didn't fall apart.

I held myself together—not with force, but with love.

And in that quiet moment, I realized:

I had become my own safe place.

ÞÞÞ

Closing Reflection

We often wait for someone else to make us feel safe.

To say, "I'm here. I won't leave. You're okay."

But the most powerful thing I've learned is this:

? You can become the person you always needed.

? You can create peace within, even when the world outside is unsteady.

? You can be your own soft place to land.

Not overnight. Not perfectly.

But tenderly. Consistently.

Lovingly.

And that is the greatest safety of all.

ÞÞÞ

✍? *Journaling Prompt*

When do I feel emotionally safe?

What words, spaces, or actions help me feel protected and comforted?

How can I give more of that to myself this week?

6

Chapter 6: Redefining Success in Solitude

There's a kind of stillness that only solitude offers. At first, it felt suffocating—like I had been cut off from the world. But slowly, I began to notice something underneath the quiet: the soft voice of my soul asking me a question I had never taken seriously before.

"What does success mean to you—if no one else is watching?"

For the first time in my adult life, I didn't have a job, a calendar packed with commitments, or people expecting things from me. And that terrified me. Because somewhere deep inside, I had linked my worth to my output. If I wasn't busy, earning, achieving, being praised—was I still valuable?

That was the real struggle. Not just being without a title or a plan—but feeling like I had lost a piece of my identity.

And that's where the shift began.

❧❧❧

The Old Success Script

We're all handed a script for success. Usually early in life.
It goes something like this:

Study hard.
Get into a good college.
Land a respectable job.
Earn well.
Find a life partner.
Buy a house.
Be busy (and make it look effortless).
Repeat until retirement.

I followed this script with loyalty, thinking that ticking these boxes would bring me happiness. And for a while, it did. Or at least it gave me the illusion of direction. Until one day, life interrupted that script—unexpectedly and completely.

And in that interruption, I had space to ask:

"What if the script isn't mine?"

ᐅᐅᐅ

Solitude as a Mirror

The most beautiful—and brutal—thing about solitude is that it shows you what you've been avoiding.

With no deadlines to chase and no one around to distract me, I began sitting with myself in long, quiet moments. At first, I tried to fill the silence: reading, scrolling, rearranging things around the house. But eventually, the noise of distraction faded, and something inside whispered gently:

"You've been moving so fast to *feel* valuable...
you haven't stopped to *know* yourself."

In that pause, I saw a clearer version of me—someone who wasn't defined by job titles or external validation. Someone with dreams I had buried under expectations. Someone who wanted peace, depth, and honesty more than applause.

ᐅᐅᐅ

New Definitions of Success

As I let go of the old script, I began to create a new one—one that felt aligned, soulful, and personal.

I began defining success not by how much I *achieved*, but by how fully I *lived*.

? A calm nervous system.
? Reading something that opened my heart.
??♀? Time spent journaling instead of doom-scrolling.
? A day where I didn't betray my own needs.
? Choosing rest over guilt.
? Creating something, even if no one else saw it.

These small things were never celebrated in the world I came from. But they meant everything to the woman I was becoming.

ՖՖՖ

From Productivity to Presence

I used to feel guilty on slow days. Like I was wasting time. Like I needed to *prove* I was still valuable by staying productive.

But solitude helped me question:

Why is rest shameful? Why is doing less seen as laziness?

And so I began honoring *presence* as a form of power.

Instead of measuring my day by how many tasks I completed, I asked:

- Was I kind to myself today?
- Did I breathe deeply at least once?
- Did I do one thing that made my heart feel alive?

Presence isn't loud. It doesn't earn trophies.
But it grounds you in a way productivity never can.

ՖՖՖ

Embracing Slowness

One morning, I made tea and just stood by the window—watching the leaves sway. It lasted maybe ten minutes. But something about that moment felt sacred. I wasn't rushing. I wasn't scrolling. I wasn't performing.

I was *living*.
And I felt—peaceful.

In that moment, I understood that slowness isn't the opposite of success. It's the soil where true purpose can grow.

Solitude gave me the gift of slowing down. Of doing one thing at a time. Of savoring. And I realized: maybe success isn't a race. Maybe it's a rhythm.

ᐅᐅᐅ

Purpose, Not Pressure

In those quiet hours alone, I started reading again. Writing again. Learning things I always said I was "too busy" for. And without even trying, I began feeling purposeful again—but not in the way the world taught me.

My purpose wasn't about performance.
It was about connection—first to myself, then to what felt meaningful.

I asked myself:

- What lights me up inside?
- What makes me lose track of time?
- What does my soul keep returning to?

And I followed those threads gently. Slowly. Without rushing to monetize them or turn them into goals. Just *being* with what moved me.

That was enough.

ᐅᐅᐅ

Depth Over Display

One of the most healing realizations was this:
I don't need to prove my worth to anyone anymore.
    Not on social media.
Not in conversations.
Not through status updates or productivity.
    I used to chase a version of success that looked good to others.
Now I chase a version that *feels* good to me.
    The quiet wins mean the most:

- The day I forgave myself for a mistake.
- The moment I felt proud of my growth without needing to post about it.
- The hour I spent dancing in my room alone, just for the joy of it.

These don't earn applause. But they build something unshakable inside.

ᐅᐅᐅ

Everyday Success

Success no longer lives in a faraway future.
    It lives in my daily life:

- In choosing foods that nourish me.
- In showing up for myself with honesty.
- In creating something beautiful and imperfect.
- In trusting the process—even when there's no clear end.

I still have dreams. I still work hard. But I've redefined what matters.
And in that shift, I've found a gentler, truer version of success.
One that doesn't burn me out.
One that doesn't make me abandon myself.
One that feels like *coming home.*

ᗷᗷᗷ

? *Closing Reflection*

I used to think success was something I had to *reach.*
Now I see it's something I can *live*—right here, right now.
I don't need more money, titles, or followers to feel whole.
I just need alignment. Peace. Presence. And the courage to trust my own rhythm.
And maybe that's what real success is:
To wake up in a life you don't need to escape.
To feel safe inside your own heart.
To honor who you're becoming—even if no one else claps for it.

ᗷᗷᗷ

? *Journaling Prompt*

If I defined success by my own values—not society's—what would it look like?
How would I spend my time?
What would I stop chasing?
What small wins am I proud of today?

7

Chapter 7: Reconnecting with My Body

I didn't realize how long I had been living outside of my body—until I finally came home to it.

It was subtle at first. A quiet ache in my lower back. A stiffness in my shoulders that I brushed off. A tiredness I kept ignoring. For years, I moved through life like a floating mind, disconnected from the very vessel that carried me through everything.

Solitude brought me back.

Not because I planned it.

But because in the stillness, there was nowhere else to run.

ʕʕʕ

The Silence of Neglect

For the longest time, I treated my body like a machine.

Sleep when there's time.

Eat whatever's fastest.

Keep going—no matter what.

I didn't do this because I hated my body.

I did it because I was taught to prioritize everything else. Deadlines. Appearances. Hustle. Approval.

In those early quiet weeks of solitude, my body spoke up in ways I hadn't noticed before.

A hollow stomach I ignored.

A shallow breath I held for too long.

A heaviness in my chest that no amount of scrolling could numb.

And one day, it hit me:

"You've been here for me through it all... and I haven't really been here for you."

ppp

Learning to Listen

Listening to my body wasn't a skill I had.

I had been taught to override it.

Push through pain.

Ignore fatigue.

Suppress hunger.

Tighten your stomach. Smile. Don't show too much softness.

But now, in solitude, there was space to pause.

And that pause became sacred.

I started asking simple questions:

- "What do you need today?"
- "What are you holding that I haven't acknowledged?"
- "Where does it hurt when I'm anxious?"

And without fail, my body answered—with tension, cravings, warmth, fatigue, lightness.

It had always been speaking. I had just stopped listening.

ppp

Movement Without Punishment

I used to move my body to "burn calories" or "earn rest."

Now, I move it because it feels good to *be alive.*

Walking slowly in the morning sunlight.

Stretching in bed before sleep.

Dancing barefoot in my room to songs that remind me I am not broken.

No timers. No guilt. No goals.

Just joy.

Just breath.

Just movement that feels like love, not punishment.

ᑭᑭᑭ

Nourishment Over Control

My relationship with food had always been tricky.

Eat "clean." Avoid carbs. Feel guilty. Start over.

But in solitude, I asked my body what she really needed. And the answer surprised me.

Sometimes it was warm soup and a pasta salad.

Other times, it was banana cake and childhood comfort.

Instead of judging my cravings, I began honoring them.

I stopped eating with shame.

I started eating with reverence.

I lit a candle. Slowed down. Gave thanks.

And food became holy again.

ᑭᑭᑭ

Reclaiming My Body Image

There was a time when mirrors felt like enemies.

I would look and only see flaws—some tanning, acne spot or an active pimple.

But now, I see strength.
I see softness.
I see the shape of survival.

This body has carried me through heartbreak, grief, long nights of crying, and moments of pure joy. She's been my home—even when I refused to decorate her with love.

I now choose to wear clothes that feel like a hug.
I speak to my reflection with kindness.
And when I don't feel beautiful, I remind myself: *beauty was never the point—being real was.*

ϷϷϷ

Creating Rituals of Care

Healing my relationship with my body became a ritual—daily, gentle, intentional.

In the mornings, I oil my skin with slow hands and gratitude.
At night, I stretch in silence and listen to the rhythm of my breath.
I touch my heartbeat and say: *"Hey, I Love You more. You're safe now."*

These rituals are not about luxury. They are about *presence.*

I'm not waiting for a special day to treat my body with care.
Today *is* the special day.

ϷϷϷ

The Sacredness of Embodiment

The deeper I came into my body, the closer I felt to something divine.

Walking barefoot on grass.
Breathing in sync with the rising sun.
Lying under the sky and realizing: I am made of the same elements.

This body is not just skin and bones.
It is a temple of intuition.

A container of stories.
A map of memories.
A sacred space where soul meets earth.

ϷϷϷ

Moments That Healed Me

There were no grand epiphanies—just quiet, gentle moments that stitched me back together.

- Laughing so hard I forgot my sadness.
- Holding my belly while I cried, instead of sucking it in.
- Eating with joy instead of shame.
- Taking naps in the middle of the day because *rest is my right.*

And one night, looking in the mirror and whispering:
"Thank you for never giving up on me."

ϷϷϷ

What I Know Now

My body is not an enemy.
It's not a project.
It's not a before-and-after photo.
It is my partner.
My protector.
My truth-teller.
It deserves softness, slowness, and songs sung into the silence.
Every step I take now is not just about healing—it's about honoring the body that carried me through the storm.

ϷϷϷ

? Journaling Prompts

- When do I feel most alive in my body?
- What do I want to thank my body for?
- What is one way I can reconnect with my body today?

ᗡᗡᗡ

? Final Reflection

We live in a world that teaches us to be at war with our bodies.

But healing begins the moment we choose peace.

To anyone reading this who has ever felt distant from their own body—may this chapter remind you:

Your body is not a problem to be solved.

It is a miracle waiting to be loved.

8

Chapter 8: Making Peace with Uncertainty

Some days, it felt like I was walking through fog with no map, no compass, and no clear destination. There were mornings I'd wake up and wonder—*What now? What next? When will life finally make sense?*

The silence of not knowing was loud.

The waiting was weighty.

And the unknown often felt like a cliff I was trying not to fall off.

I used to crave certainty like air. I thought if I could just have answers—about work, love, the future—I'd finally feel safe. But when life paused, when things didn't go as I planned, and when I found myself alone with no clear "next," I realized I had no choice but to befriend the unknown.

♡♡♡

The Fear of Not Knowing

There's a quiet fear that creeps in when you don't have a job, a partner, or a plan. It whispers:

You're falling behind.

Everyone else knows what they're doing.

You should have figured this out by now.

I would scroll through social media and see people with careers, families, dream vacations, busy lives. Meanwhile, I was alone in my apartment, eating dinner in silence, trying to make peace with the fact that I had no idea what was coming next.

I wasn't just uncertain—I was ashamed of being uncertain. Like I was failing at life simply because I didn't have an answer.

ᗭᗭᗭ

What Control Meant to Me

Before solitude, I lived in a cycle of over planning.
Every day had a to-do list.
Every month had a vision board.
Every moment was optimized for progress.
    It looked like discipline.
It felt like safety.
But deep down, it was fear in disguise.
    Fear of failing.
Fear of wasting time.
Fear of becoming irrelevant or forgotten.
    Control gave me a sense of order, but not peace.
It kept me busy but not fulfilled.
    So when life stopped following my plans—when things unraveled and the old maps didn't work anymore—I broke down.
    And then, quietly, I broke open.

ᗭᗭᗭ

The Moment I Let Go

One morning, I woke up and didn't have the energy to "figure it out."
No more vision boards. No more strategies.
Just... concord.

I made tea. I sat in silence. I let the questions float without answering them.

And in that placidity, something shifted.

It wasn't clarity. It wasn't a breakthrough.

It was a whisper:

"You don't have to know everything. You just have to be here."

That whisper became my lifeline.

ϷϷϷ

Living in the In-Between

There's a strange, sacred space between who you were and who you're becoming.

A liminal space. An in-between. A cocoon.

In this space, I wasn't defined by a title, a timeline, or a relationship.

I was just *me*—raw, uncertain, unfolding.

It was uncomfortable at first.

But slowly, I stopped resisting it.

And started respecting it.

Because here's what I realized:

The in-between isn't nothing.

It's where everything begins to shift.

ϷϷϷ

Little Anchors of Stability

To stay grounded in uncertainty, I created small certainties:

- A cup of warm lemon water every morning
- A playlist of songs that reminded me I'm not alone
- A journal where I could pour my fears without judgment
- A half an hour walks outside—even when I didn't feel like it

These little anchors reminded me that while I couldn't control the big picture, I could hold on to moments of steadiness. And sometimes, that's enough.

ᚹᚹᚹ

Learning from Nature

One afternoon, I was sitting under a tree, watching its leaves dance in the breeze. It hit me—this tree doesn't worry about what's next.

It grows in seasons.
It sheds what it no longer needs.
It trusts that new leaves will come.

Nature is never in a hurry, yet everything gets done.
I began to believe the same could be true for me.

ᚹᚹᚹ

Redefining Safety

I used to think safety meant having a plan.

Now, I believe safety means trusting myself—especially when the plan falls apart.

Safety is knowing that even if I don't have all the answers, I have *me*.
My breath.
My resilience.
My inner compass.

Uncertainty no longer felt like a threat.
It became an invitation—to trust deeper, to grow slowly, to surrender softly.

ᚹᚹᚹ

Quiet Transformations

As the weeks passed, things didn't magically fall into place. But *I* did.
I wasn't waking up in panic anymore.
I started saying "I don't know" without shame.
I smiled more. Worried less. Breathed deeper.
I became someone who could sit with the unknown—and still feel whole.

🜙🜙🜙

What I Know Now

Uncertainty is not the enemy.
It's the space between the old story and the new beginning.
It's uncomfortable, yes.
But it's also honest.
And honest space is where true growth lives.
Some of the most beautiful chapters in my life began when I had no idea what was next.
I now believe:
The unknown is not empty.
It's *full*—of possibility, transformation, and unexpected grace.

🜙🜙🜙

? Journaling Prompts

- What uncertainties am I resisting right now?
- What would it feel like to stop fighting the unknown and start flowing with it?
- In what ways has uncertainty helped me grow into a more grounded version of myself?

ᐅᐅᐅ

? Final Reflection

To the one navigating the fog—
You are not lost.
You are simply on a path that hasn't fully revealed itself.
    Keep walking.
Keep breathing.
Keep showing up for your life, even when the road ahead feels unclear.
    You don't need to know everything.
You just need to trust that what is meant for you... will never miss you.

9

Chapter 9: Finding Joy in the Ordinary

There was a time when I believed joy had to be earned—like a reward after a big achievement. It came dressed in glitter: a job offer, a romantic milestone, a new beginning. I kept looking for it in places I hadn't yet reached, imagining it would only arrive once everything fell into place.

But during my quiet days of solitude, stripped of plans, people, and performance—I stumbled upon something surprising.

Joy hadn't disappeared.
It had only changed form.
It was no longer loud. It was... subtle.
Whispering through small things I'd once overlooked.

❧❧❧

The Myth of "Big Happiness"

We grow up believing happiness must be grand.
Like a big party.
A viral post.
An award.
A wedding.

A life that looks amazing from the outside.
    And so, we wait.
We wait for holidays to feel relaxed,
for success to feel enough,
for love to finally make us whole.
    But here's what I've learned:
Waiting for joy is a way to miss it.
Because it's *already here*—just wearing quieter clothes.

ᐳᐳᐳ

A Shift in Perspective

When life slowed down, so did my gaze.
    I stopped scanning the horizon for the next big thing.
And I began to notice what was right in front of me:
    The way the sunlight spilled onto my floor in the morning.
The first sip of chai, warming my throat and calming my nerves.
A playlist from my teenage years that still knew how to comfort me.
    It wasn't dramatic.
It wasn't social media worthy.
But it was *real*.
    Joy didn't need to impress anyone anymore.
It just needed to *be felt*.

ᐳᐳᐳ

Everyday Moments That Lit Me Up

- **The smell of rain on dry earth.** I paused everything to inhale it deeply.
- **The first stretch after waking up.** My body greeting itself gently.
- **Lighting a candle at night.** No reason. Just because it made me smile.

- **My favorite pajamas,** soft and worn, like a hug from my past self.
- **A growing sapling.** Pure, contagious delight.
- **The click of my pen on a fresh page.** A small promise of new thoughts.

These weren't things I could add to a résumé.
But they added something precious to my life: presence.

ᗖᗖᗖ

The Joy Journal

One day, I began writing down one joyful moment before bed.
   At first, it felt silly. What could possibly be joyful in a day spent mostly alone?
   But I did it anyway:

- "Saw a butterfly outside my window."
- "Tried a new soup recipe—turned out delicious."
- "Listened to an old love song and danced in the kitchen."
- "Spoke kindly to myself today."

The more I wrote, the more I *noticed*.
And the more I noticed, the more joy seemed to grow.
   Because joy isn't always *found*—sometimes, it's simply *seen*.

ᗖᗖᗖ

Redefining Productivity

In this solitude, I began to ask myself:
What if just being... is enough?
   I wasn't building a brand.
I wasn't hitting milestones.
But I was healing. Softening. Becoming more *me*.

I started to redefine what it meant to "do something with my day."

Some days, that looked like:

- Resting when I was tired
- Listening deeply to my emotions
- Cleaning my space with intention
- Reading something that made my heart open

These were invisible acts. But they were acts of self-respect. And that, I learned, is deeply productive.

ᑭᑭᑭ

The Joy of Doing Things for Myself

There's a certain sweetness in showing up for yourself.

I began cooking just for me—not out of duty, but as a form of creativity.

I arranged flowers in an old jar, just to make my windowsill smile.

I wore lipstick at home, not because anyone would see me, but because I felt alive in it.

These small things reminded me:

I don't need a witness to matter.

I don't need an audience to be worthy of beauty.

When I began giving joy to myself, I stopped waiting for others to deliver it.

ᑭᑭᑭ

Being Present with the Present

I slowed down. I stopped multitasking. I began to listen—with my eyes, my hands, my breath.

I ate my meals without distractions.
I walked with nothing in my ears.
I sat with my tea and watched the world go by.
At first, it felt empty.
But soon, it felt *rich*.
The kind of richness that doesn't need applause.
The kind that simply says:
"This moment is enough. You are enough."

ৡৡৡ

Healing Through Lightness

I thought healing would always be heavy—tears, shadow work, deep introspection.
But sometimes, healing came through lightness.
In laughter.
Picturing little things that made me happy.
In playing with colors, textures, spices, ideas.
These small joys didn't erase my grief, but they made space around it.
They softened the edges.
They reminded me I was still alive—and still allowed to feel good.
Joy, I realized, wasn't disrespectful to my struggle.
It was a sign that the struggle hadn't stolen me.

ৡৡৡ

What I Know Now

Ecstasy doesn't have to be rare.
It doesn't have to be earned.
And it definitely doesn't need to be perfect.
It just needs to be *noticed*.

The ordinary is not empty.
It's overflowing.
And once you begin to see it,
you'll wonder how you ever missed it.

ᗷᗷᗷ

✍? Journaling Prompts

· What three small things brought me comfort today?
· Where have I overlooked joy because I was waiting for something bigger?
· How can I bring more playfulness, softness, or celebration into my daily life?

? Final Reflection

If you are in a season where life feels uneventful or "too quiet," let me tell you this:
There is magic in this pause.
There is beauty in this breath.
There is joy in this ordinary day.
You don't need to go anywhere else.
Joy is already here.
In your cup, in your breath, in your heartbeat.
The question is—
Will you pause long enough to feel it?

10

Chapter 10: Coming Home to Myself

There is a kind of home that doesn't have walls.
It doesn't have doors, or lights, or furniture.
It's made of breath.
Of trust.
Of knowing.
It lives within you—waiting, patiently, for your return.
This is not the kind of home anyone else can build for you.
You cannot buy it, marry into it, or stumble upon it.
You grow into it.
You make space for it.
And one day, often when you least expect it,
you realize:
You have come home. To yourself.

❦❦❦

The Longing That Started It All

I began this journey not with a plan—but with a longing.
It was quiet but aching.
I wanted love, certainty, direction.

I wanted to feel chosen. Whole. Alive.

At the time, I believed I was waiting for something or someone to arrive.

But what I didn't realize then was this:

That longing wasn't about someone else.

It was my soul calling *me* back home.

I thought I had lost everything.

But truly, I was being invited to meet myself—again, and for the first time.

ᗡᗡᗡ

What Solitude Taught Me

Alone time isn't easy.

It stretches you.

It shows you all the parts of yourself you've ignored, buried, or outsourced to others.

But it also reveals your gold.

In solitude, I discovered I was braver than I knew.

I learned to sit with my sadness without trying to silence it.

I found comfort in my own breath, calm in my own presence.

I wasn't as broken as I feared.

I was just unfamiliar to myself.

And slowly, through every quiet morning and tearful night,

I got to know the woman within.

ᗡᗡᗡ

Letting Go of Old Narratives

There were stories I had carried for far too long:

- "I'm only worthy if I'm useful."
- "I have to earn love by being perfect."

- "I must always be strong, no matter what."

But healing asked me to loosen my grip.
To stop performing and start *being*.
To let go of who I thought I had to be—and allow who I truly was to emerge.
In that surrender, I found space.
Not just to breathe—but to *be seen*—by myself.
And I liked what I saw.

ᐲᐲᐲ

Redefining Self-Love

I used to think self-love meant bubble baths and affirmations.
Now I know it means:

- Holding my own hand when I feel afraid
- Saying "no" without guilt
- Forgiving myself for the moments I didn't know better
- Feeding my body like it deserves to thrive
- Letting myself rest—not because I've earned it, but because I *need* it

Self-love is not loud or glamorous.
It is steady. Compassionate. Fierce in its softness.
It is not a reward. It is a right.

ᐲᐲᐲ

Integrating All the Selves I've Been

As I healed, I stopped rejecting my past selves.
The anxious girl who couldn't sleep?
She was trying to protect me.

The woman who waited for a text that never came?
She loved deeply. That was never a weakness.
The version of me that broke down?
She cracked open to let the light in.
I began to gather all these selves into one embrace.
Not to fix them—but to thank them.
Because every one of them led me here.

ᗡᗡᗡ

Coming Home in My Body, Mind, and Spirit

This chapter of my life didn't come with applause or announcements.
There was no final achievement, no big epiphany.
Just a moment—quiet and tender—when I realized:
I no longer needed to escape myself.
I could sit still, feel safe.
I could look in the mirror and meet kind eyes.
I could wake up and not dread the day.
I could walk alone and feel whole.
This was the home I had been seeking all along.

ᗡᗡᗡ

Signs I'm No Longer Waiting to Be Saved

I stop reaching for what doesn't reach back

- I trust my body when it says "rest"
- I create my bliss without needing permission
- I build a life that feels *good*—not just looks good
- I'm okay with being misunderstood—because I understand *myself*

Coming home is not a one-time arrival.
It is a daily devotion.
It is a choice to return—to love, to trust, to presence.
And I choose it now, again and again.

ppp

A Letter to the Woman I've Become

Dear Me,
You didn't just survive.
You softened and grew.
You chose yourself again and again, even when it hurt.
You walked through uncertainty, and still made space for joy.
You learned how to hold yourself with both hands.
You found your voice—and used it gently, bravely.
I am so proud of you.
Not because you became someone new—
But because you remembered who you've always been.
With all my love,
You.

ppp

Closing Gratitude: To Solitude, To Self

To the nights I cried and the mornings I tried again—thank you.
To the version of me who kept walking even when it was hard—thank you.
To the stillness that taught me how to listen—thank you.
This journey was not about finding a new self.
It was about *coming home* to the one who had been waiting inside me all along.

ppp

✍? Final Journaling Prompts

- What does "home" feel like to me—not as a place, but as a state of being?
- How have I changed through this season of solitude and self-focus?
- What parts of myself am I ready to cherish, protect, and grow?

ᗷᗷᗷ

? Final Reflection

This chapter is not the end.
It is a new beginning—a softer, stronger, and more honest one.
    You are not behind.
You are not broken.
You are simply *becoming*.
    And in the becoming, you are already home.
    Let this be your reminder:
    You are your own safe place.
Your own soft landing.
Your own light.
    Keep returning to her.
Keep loving her.
Keep walking with her.
    Because *you* are the love story you've been waiting for.

"Success is not about being known by the world. It's about being deeply known by your own soul."
— *Author Unknown*

ᚦᚦᚦ

"The moment you stop chasing someone else's dream is the moment you start living your own."
— *Manali Raj (optional attribution to yourself)*

ᚦᚦᚦ

"You are not behind in life. You are exactly where your healing needs you to be."
— *Nikita Gill*

ᚦᚦᚦ

"Solitude isn't loneliness—it's sacred space to meet yourself without noise or judgment."
— *Brianna Wiest*

ᚦᚦᚦ

"Rest is not a reward for success. Rest is part of it."
— *Alexandra Elle*

ᚦᚦᚦ

"You were never meant to be constantly busy. You were meant to feel deeply, grow slowly, and bloom quietly."
— *Unknown*

ᚦᚦᚦ

"Redefine success as this: waking up with peace in your chest and honesty in your choices."
— *Manali Raj*

$$\nu\nu\nu$$

"In the echo of an empty room, I found the echo of myself I had long abandoned.

    Not a saviour, not a crowd – Just Me

    And that's the beginning. "

$$\nu\nu\nu$$

"The detour of my life isn't a delay, It's a re-route to something better."

$$\nu\nu\nu$$

"I am gradually becoming a reason for someone to believe again – "
What a beautiful purpose.""

$$\nu\nu\nu$$

"Some days healing looks like doing nothing.

    And, that's completely okay. "

$$\nu\nu\nu$$

"I saw her;

    The girl I used to be.

    And whispered ...

    Thank you for surviving."

$$\nu\nu\nu$$

"Broken seasons aren't the end of the story. The timeline is still beautiful."

$$\nu\nu\nu$$

"Real closure is being okay with unfinished endings, messy conclusions and words left unsaid."

$$\nu\nu\nu$$

"I release what once felt like forever and make room for the miracles still on their way"

❧❧❧

— Manali Raj

www.ingramcontent.com/pod-product-compliance
Lightning Source LLC
Chambersburg PA
CBHW020457160726
47991CB00007B/2701